Ramadan for Toddlers and Kids Book for Kids: Activity Islamic Book

Giza, Egypt,
Zip Code 12555
https://dr-adel.site
E-mail: adelmam55@gmail.com

This Book Belongs to:

Name: - - - - - - - - - - - -

Address: - - - - - - - - - -

Preface

Ramadan for Toddlers and Kids is a magic coloring book including more than fifty fantastic illustrations for you and your kids to color. Be swept away right into a religious world where spiritual, Islamic-type spirits, playful Ramadan witches, and time magic overflows. This is a grown-up coloring publication, yet older kids and adults would certainly likewise appreciate it. There are no repeat designs on any page. You will love this book as informative and relaxing coloring pages. Every page you color will pull you into a relaxing world where your responsibilities will seem to fade away.

- A perfect gift for kids and adults with many beautiful illustrations
- Hours of incredible inspiration, meditation and fun
- 50 fantastic inducing designs
- Good quality white paper
- Best for paints, crayons, colored pencils, watercolor, and light fine tip markers
- Extra large size (8.5" x 11")
- 100 pages
- Beautiful design
- One-sided printed pages with many Quaranic Verses and Quotations in the opposite page.
- Ramadan calendar for the year 2021 is included.

Adel M Abdel-Azim

Please, test your coloring pen on this page to see how it reacts with the type of this paper. Also, please put one or two blank papers behind each page as you color to guard against bleeding of ink into the following page.

Ramadan Calender
Ramadan Fasting and Prayer Times According to the Makkah, Saudi Arabia, Time Zone (+3)

Date	Fajr	Sunrise	Zhuhr	Asr	Maghrib	Isha
01 Ramadan, 1442 (13 April, 2021)	5:01	6:03	12:21	15:45	18:39	19:42
02 Ramadan, 1442 (14 April, 2021)	5:00	6:02	12:21	15:45	18:40	19:42
03 Ramadan, 1442 (15 April, 2021)	4:59	6:01	12:21	15:44	18:40	19:43
04 Ramadan, 1442 (16 April, 2021)	4:58	6:01	12:20	15:44	18:40	19:43
05 Ramadan, 1442 (17 April, 2021)	4:57	6:00	12:20	15:44	18:41	19:44
06 Ramadan, 1442 (18 April, 2021)	4:56	5:59	12:20	15:43	18:41	19:44
07 Ramadan, 1442 (19 April, 2021)	4:55	5:58	12:20	15:43	18:41	19:45
08 Ramadan, 1442 (20 April, 2021)	4:54	5:57	12:19	15:43	18:42	19:45
09 Ramadan, 1442 (21 April, 2021)	4:53	5:57	12:19	15:42	18:42	19:46
10 Ramadan, 1442 (22 April, 2021)	4:52	5:56	12:19	15:42	18:42	19:46
11 Ramadan, 1442 (23 April, 2021)	4:52	5:55	12:19	15:41	18:43	19:47
12 Ramadan, 1442 (24 April, 2021)	4:51	5:54	12:19	15:41	18:43	19:47
13 Ramadan, 1442 (25 April, 2021)	4:50	5:54	12:19	15:41	18:44	19:48
14 Ramadan, 1442 (26 April, 2021)	4:49	5:53	12:18	15:40	18:44	19:48
15 Ramadan, 1442 (27 April, 2021)	4:48	5:52	12:18	15:40	18:44	19:49
16 Ramadan, 1442 (28 April, 2021)	4:47	5:52	12:18	15:39	18:45	19:49
17 Ramadan, 1442 (29 April, 2021)	4:47	5:51	12:18	15:39	18:45	19:50
18 Ramadan, 1442 (30 April, 2021)	4:46	5:50	12:18	15:39	18:46	19:50
19 Ramadan, 1442 (01 May, 2021)	4:45	5:50	12:18	15:38	18:46	19:51
20 Ramadan, 1442 (02 May, 2021)	4:44	5:49	12:18	15:38	18:46	19:51
21 Ramadan, 1442 (03 May, 2021)	4:43	5:48	12:17	15:38	18:47	19:52
22 Ramadan, 1442 (04 May, 2021)	4:43	5:48	12:17	15:37	18:47	19:52
23 Ramadan, 1442 (05 May, 2021)	4:42	5:47	12:17	15:37	18:48	19:53
24 Ramadan, 1442 (06 May, 2021)	4:41	5:47	12:17	15:37	18:48	19:53
25 Ramadan, 1442 (07 May, 2021)	4:41	5:46	12:17	15:36	18:48	19:54
26 Ramadan, 1442 (08 May, 2021)	4:40	5:46	12:17	15:36	18:49	19:55
27 Ramadan, 1442 (09 May, 2021)	4:39	5:45	12:17	15:36	18:49	19:55
28 Ramadan, 1442 (10 May, 2021)	4:39	5:45	12:17	15:35	18:50	19:56
29 Ramadan, 1442 (11 May, 2021)	4:38	5:44	12:17	15:35	18:50	19:56
30 Ramadan, 1442 (12 May, 2021)	4:37	5:44	12:17	15:35	18:50	19:57

شَهْرُ رَمَضَانَ الَّذِى أُنزِلَ فِيهِ الْقُرْءَانُ هُدًى لِّلنَّاسِ وَبَيِّنَٰتٍ مِّنَ الْهُدَىٰ وَالْفُرْقَانِ ۚ فَمَن شَهِدَ مِنكُمُ الشَّهْرَ فَلْيَصُمْهُ ۖ وَمَن كَانَ مَرِيضًا أَوْ عَلَىٰ سَفَرٍ فَعِدَّةٌ مِّنْ أَيَّامٍ أُخَرَ ۗ يُرِيدُ اللَّهُ بِكُمُ الْيُسْرَ وَلَا يُرِيدُ بِكُمُ الْعُسْرَ وَلِتُكْمِلُوا الْعِدَّةَ وَلِتُكَبِّرُوا اللَّهَ عَلَىٰ مَا هَدَىٰكُمْ وَلَعَلَّكُمْ تَشْكُرُونَ ﴿١٨٥﴾

Chapter 2, Verse 185 in Arabic Quran.

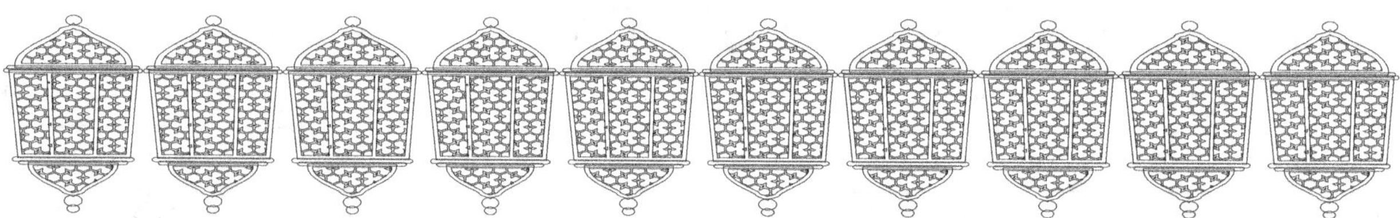

The month of Ramadan is that in which was revealed the Quran; a guidance for mankind, and clear proofs of the guidance, and the criterion (of right and wrong). And whosoever of you is present, let him fast the month, and whosoever of you is sick or on a journey, a number of other days. Allah desires for you ease; He desires not hardship for you; and that you should complete the period, and that you should magnify Allah for having guided you, and that perhaps you may be thankful.

Translated By:
The Quran: Muhammad M. Pickthall, Ed.

About Ramadan

Ramadan, which is the ninth month of the Islamic calendar, is observed by all Muslims worldwide as the month of fasting (sawm), prayer, reflection, and community. Ramadan was the month at which the first revelation to the prophet Muhammad started. The annual observance of Ramadan is considered as one of the Five Pillars of Islam and lasts from twenty-nine to thirty days, from one sighting of the crescent moon to the next.

Fasting which starts from sunrise to sunset is obligatory (fard) for all adult Muslims who are not acutely or chronically diseased, traveling a long distance, elderly, breastfeeding, menstruating, or diabetic. The predawn meal is known in Arabic as Suhur (Sohoor), and the nightly feast that breaks the fast is called Iftar. Muslims who live in territories with a midnight sun or polar night should follow the timetable of Mecca, or they can follow the timetable of the closest country in which night can be distinguished from the day.

The spiritual rewards (Thawab) of fasting are believed to be multiplied during Ramadan. Accordingly, Muslims refrain not only from food and drink but also sexual relations (at the time of fasting) tobacco products, and sinful behavior, devoting themselves instead to Salat (prayer) and recitation of the Quran.

Ramadan is known in Arabic as رَمَضَان, and also spelled Ramazan, Ramzan, Ramadhan or Ramathan. In the Persian and Turkish languages, the Arabic letter ض (Dād) is pronounced as /z/. Some Muslim countries with historical Persian and Turkish influence, such as Azerbaijan, Iran, India, Pakistan, and Turkey, use the word Ramazan or Ramzan. The word Romzan is used also in Bangladesh.

Ramadan was the time when the Qur'an was revealed to the prophet Muhammad (Peace Be Upon Him).

This is the image of the word Muhammad written in Arabic script:
Can you color the letters with beautiful different colors?

To celebrate the revelation of the holy scriptures, fasting is compulsory for all adult Muslims - except in special circumstances - on every day of this holy month.

The month lasts 29 or 30 days, depending on a sighting of the new moon to signal the start of Ramadan and then another moon sighting to determine the end of Ramadan and the start of the next month, Shawwal.

What fasting means:
Fasting means no food or drink and also abstaining from bad habits and sins such as smoking, swearing, gossipping, arguing, fighting or being disrespectful, cruel or selfish. Sexual relations are also banned during the hours of fasting.

Who fasts:
All male and female adults (meaning anyone who has undergone puberty) must take part in fasting.

This is the image of the word Muhammad written in Arabic: Can you color the letters and the frames with beautiful different colors?

Exceptions for Fasting:
There are exceptions. Anyone who is ill or traveling during Ramadan and who doesn't take part in the fasting must make up the days of fasting later.

The name Muhammad written in Thuluth, a script variety of Islamic calligraphy: Can you color the letters with beautiful different colors?

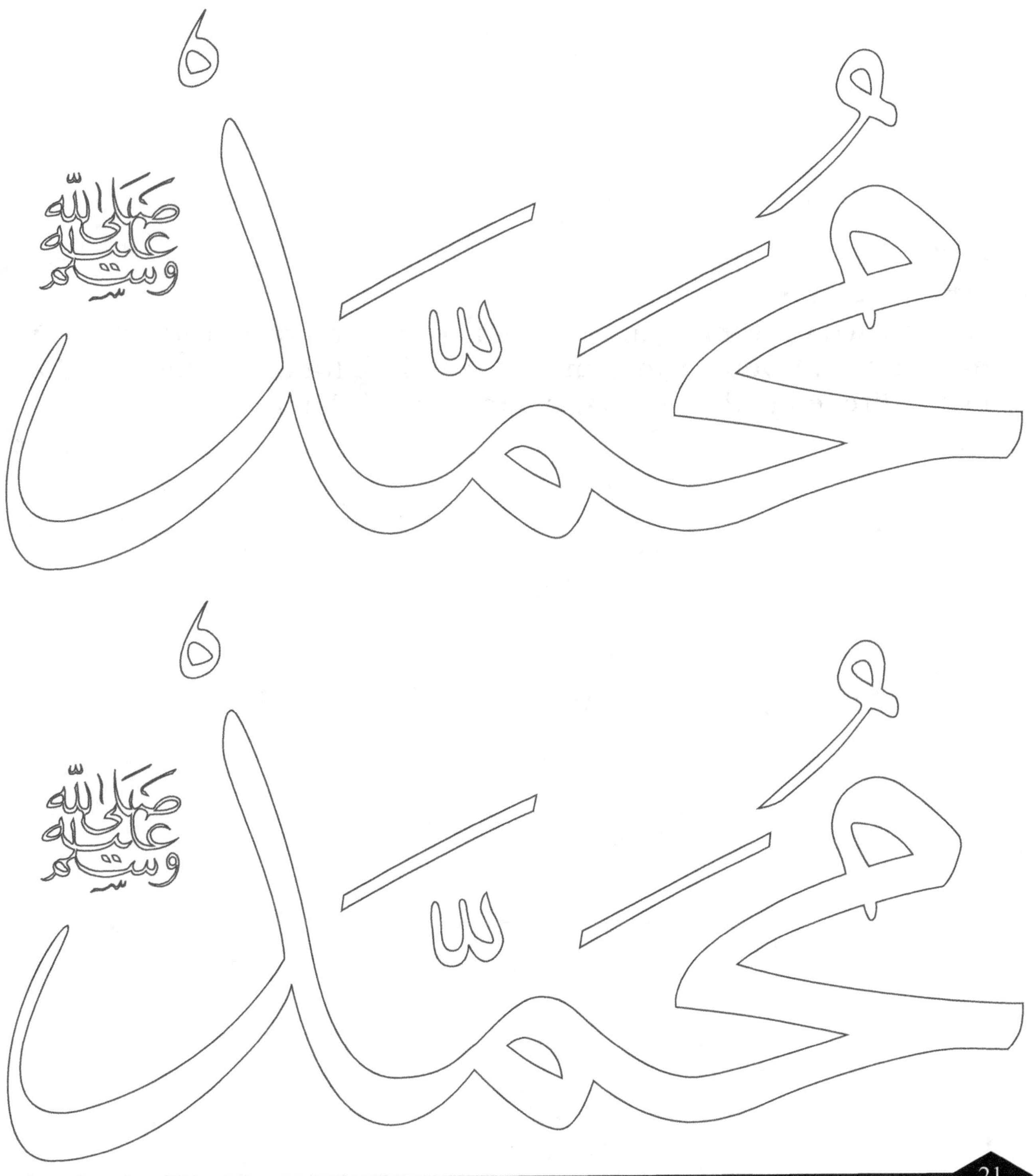

What is about Women:
Women who are pregnant, menstruating or breastfeeding don't have to fast. If you begin your period during Ramadan fasting, the fast is broken and you must make up for it later.

The name Muhammad written in Arabic script calligraphy: Can you color the letters with beautiful different colors?

How can I compensate for fasting:
Those with permanent health conditions instead help the poor to compensate for not fasting.

The name Muhammad written in Thuluth, a script variety of Islamic calligraphy: Can you color the letters with beautiful different colors?

What is about elderly or ill:
The elderly and chronically ill (including diabetics) are exempt from fasting, along with the severely mentally ill. Doctors can give advice on whether you are fit and well enough to fast.

The name Muhammad written in Thuluth, a script variety of Islamic calligraphy: Can you color the letters with beautiful different colors?

How can I make it up (fidyah):
When someone cannot fast in Ramadan and can't make up the lost days afterwards (for example, due to being elderly or because of ill health, women who are pregnant, breastfeeding or menstruating), then they should pay for someone else to be fed. This is known as fidyah.

Islamic Relief says the present rate is $5 for each day that is missed (this should provide one person with two meals or two people with one meal.) If someone misses all the fasts of Ramadan, they would need to pay $150.

The name Muhammad written in Arabic script calligraphy: Can you color the letters with beautiful different colors?

What is the meaning of Atonement (kaffarah):
Kaffarah (meaning 'penance') is the compensation you should pay if you deliberately miss or break a fast in the month of Ramadan without a valid reason.

To atone for the missed/intentionally broken fast, a person must fast continuously for 60 days.

If they are unable to do that, then they have to feed 60 poor people at a rate of £5 per person (the cost of an average meal in the UK). This amounts to £300 in kaffarah for each missed/intentionally broken fast, according to Islamic Relief.

The name Muhammad written in Arabic script calligraphy: Can you color the letters with beautiful different colors?

Vomiting and fasting:
The fast is broken if you make yourself vomit deliberately, but not if it's done suddenly or involuntarily. Do not swallow the vomit or that will definitely break the fast.
If the cause of vomiting is a disease, then you can break your fast and compensate later on by any means mentioned above.

The name Muhammad written in Arabic script calligraphy: Can you color the letters with beautiful different colors?

Happy
Ramadan

What is about children:
Pre-pubescent children are not required to fast but some of them
do it for some days, or parts of days, to train themselves in readi-
ness for Ramadan as an adult.

The name Muhammad written in Arabic script calligraphy: Can you color the letters with beautiful different colors?

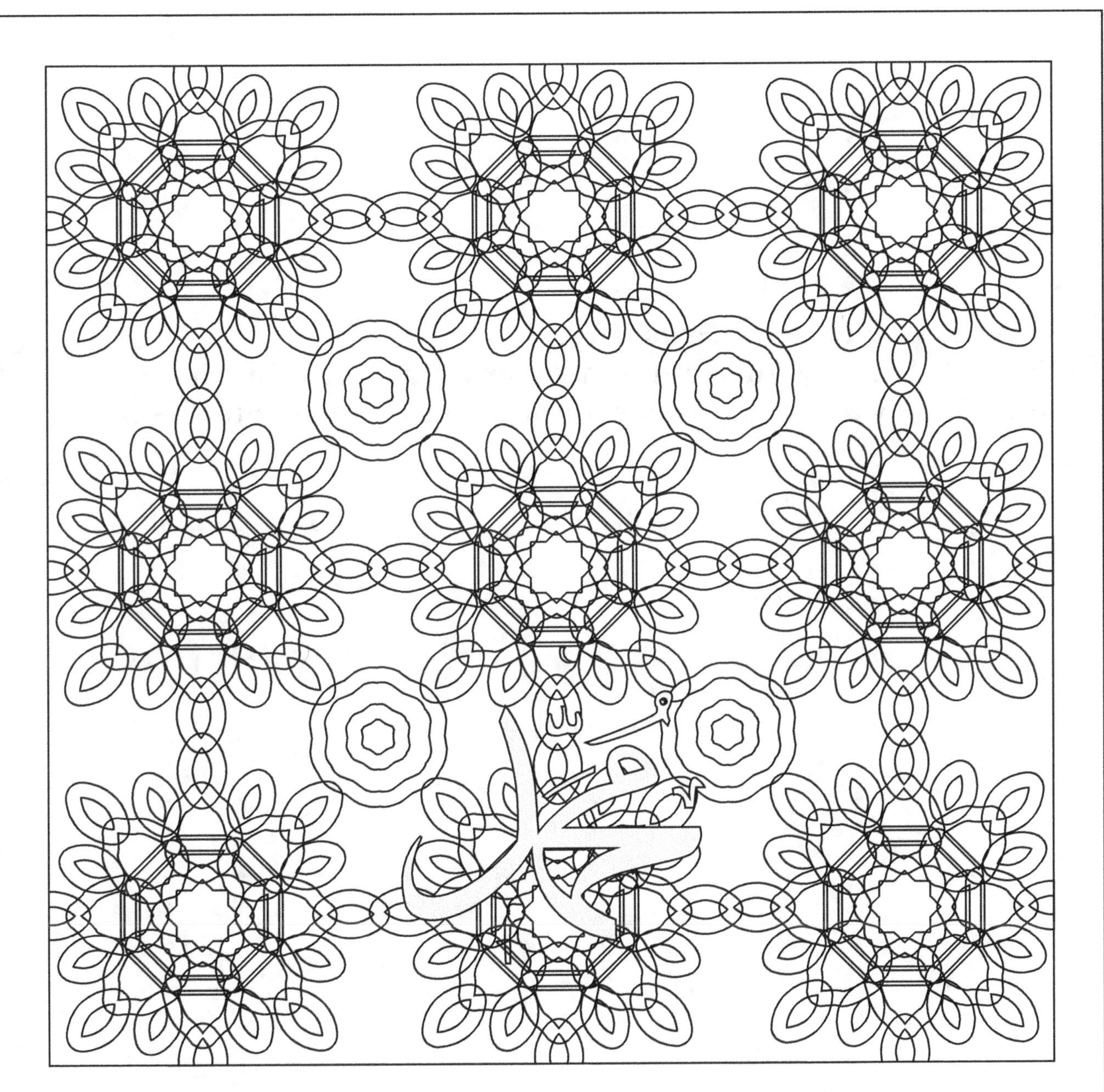

What is about teeth Brushing:
You can brush your teeth and rinse your mouth but it's not permitted to swallow any water, or you would invalidate the fast.

The name Muhammad written in Arabic script calligraphy: Can you color the letters with beautiful different colors?

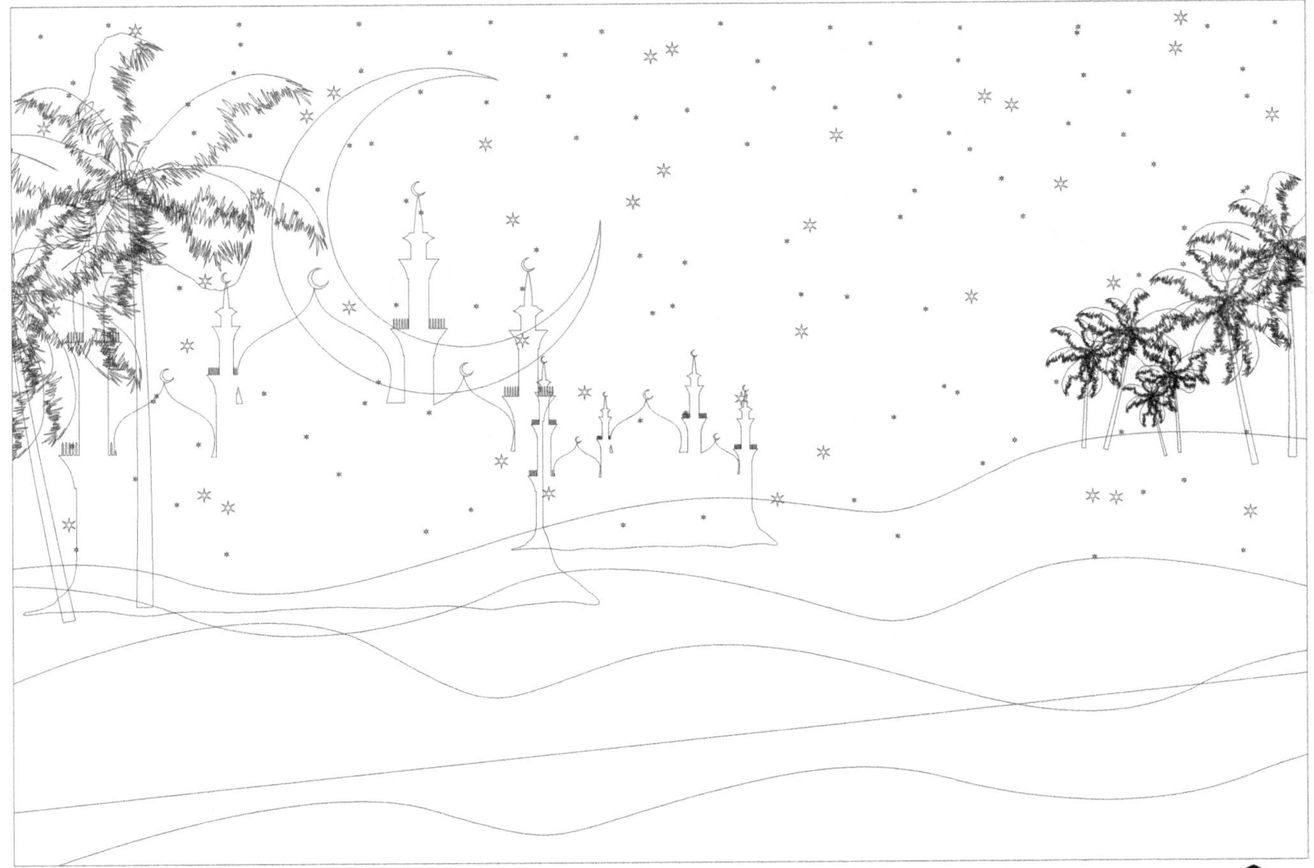

What is about Injections:
If you need injections for medical reason, it's perfectly acceptable to continue these and the fast will not be broken. If you are seriously ill, you can break your fast and compensate.

HAPPY
ISRA MI'RAJ

What is about swallowing:
Accidentally swallowing food or dust (such as airborne particles of sieved flour) or your own saliva will NOT invalidate the fast. You can also deliberately taste food, for instance if checking the seasoning when preparing a meal for the iftar later, as long as you don't swallow the food.

Happy Ramadan
Happy Ramadan

What is about purity:
You must not be in a state of janaba. This is an Islamic term meaning impurity after sex, ejaculation or the completion of the menstrual cycle. A person in this state must wash so that they can become ritually pure and take part in Ramadan fasting and prayers the following day. The full-body cleansing ritual they must undertake is known as ghusl.

THE MONTH OF
RAMADAN
IS THAT
IN WHICH WAS REVEALED
The QURAN
· A GUIDANCE ·
FOR THE PEOPLE AND CLEAR PROOFS
OF GUIDANCE AND CRITERION

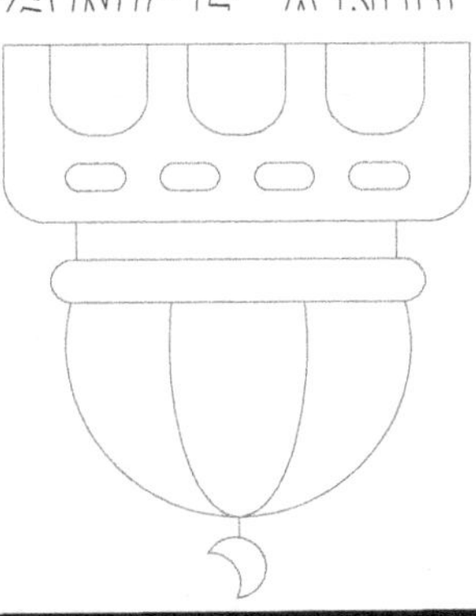

What is about eye droplets:
Eyeliner and eye drops are allowed, and drops MUST be continued if someone is suffering glaucoma. The advice is to use drops before and after the fasting and use a technique to stop the fluid draining down into the throat.

What is about music:
The Qur'an itself makes no explicit mention of music being forbidden. Some interpret a phrase "idle talks" as including singing or music, others do not.

What is about chewing gum:
You can't chew gum while fasting for Ramadan
This is because chewing gum is seen as eating and that is not allowed during the hours of fasting. Also, during chewing of gums,
sugars inside the gum can be released into your mouth.

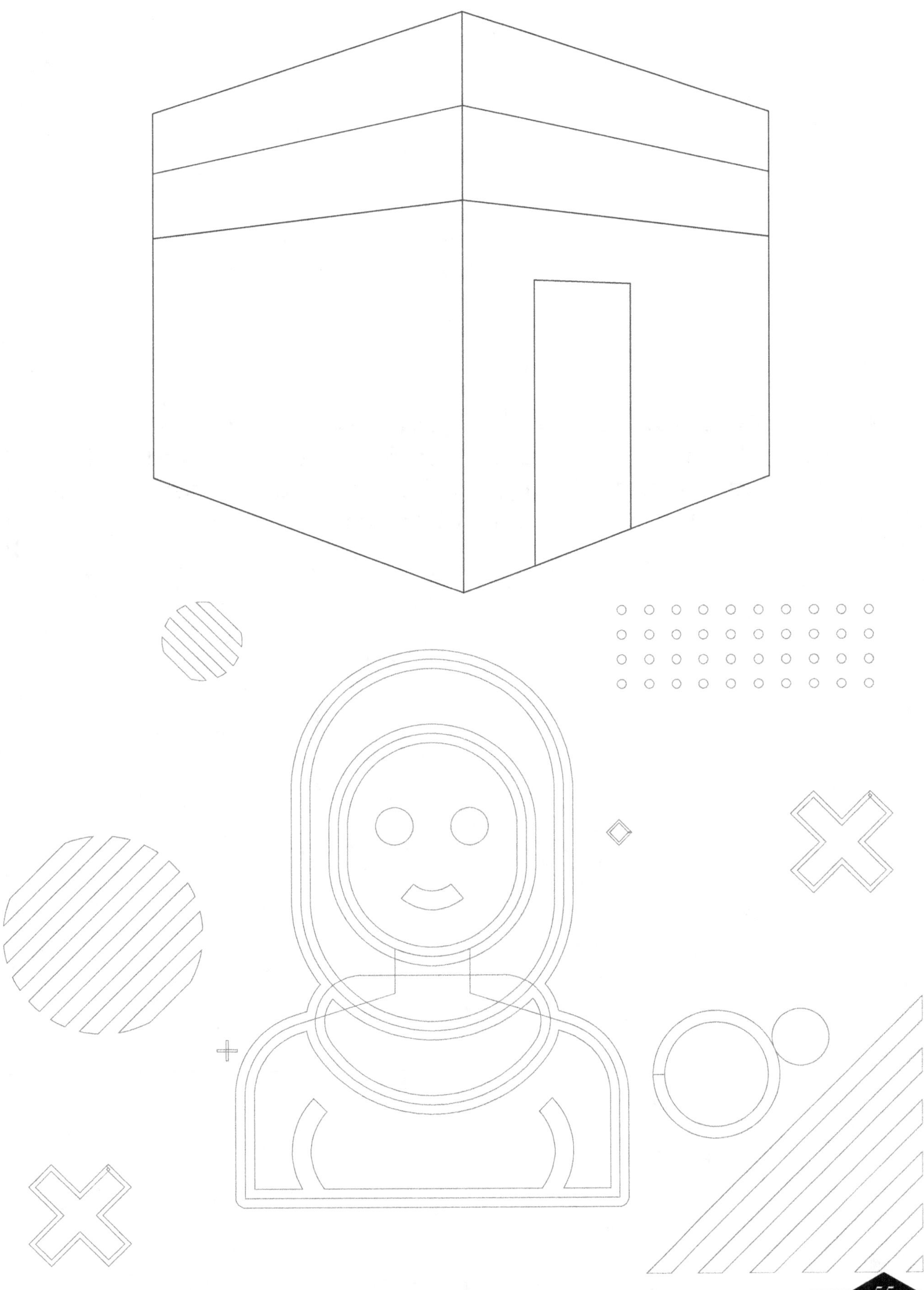

What is about asthma inhaler during Ramadan:
Asthma inhaler isn't the same as eating or drinking and is therefore permitted during fasting. In their view, people with asthma
can fast and use their inhalers whenever they need to.

What is about fitness or exercise during Ramadan:
You can exercise, but you have to plan it accordingly. It's vital to remember that your body won't have the same amount of energy that you would have on a normal day. It is advised to postpone severe exercise to be after Iftar.
Try to do light exercise like walking and meditative exercises in any spare time you have; this can help to keep the system working and blood circulating.
If you exercise within eating times, make sure you have allowed enough time for food to be digested before you exercise and that you drink plenty of water during iftar and suhoor times. Keep workouts short to between 30-60 minutes.

Always Remember:
During Ramadan, Muslims abstain from eating any food, drinking any liquids, smoking cigarettes, and engaging in any sexual activity, from dawn to sunset. That includes taking medication (even if you swallow a pill dry, without drinking any water). Chewing gum is also prohibited.

Always Remember:
Doing any of those things "invalidates" your fast for the day, and you just start over the next day. To make up for days you didn't fast, you can either fast later in the year (either all at once or a day here and there) or provide a meal to a needy person for each day you missed.

Always Remember:
Muslims are also supposed to try to curb negative thoughts and emotions like jealousy and anger, and even lesser things like swearing, complaining, and gossiping, during the month. Some people may also choose to give up or limit activities like listening to music and watching television, often in favor of listening to recitations of the Quran.

Always Remember:
When the evening call to prayer is finally made (or when the alarm on your phone's Muslim prayer app goes off), we break the day's fast with a light meal — really more of a snack — called an iftar (literally "breakfast"), before performing the evening prayer. Many also go to the mosque for the evening prayer, followed by a special prayer that is only recited during Ramadan.
This is usually followed by a larger meal a bit later in the evening, which is often shared with family and friends in one another's homes throughout the month. Then it's off to bed for a few hours of sleep before it's time to wake up and start all over again.

Always Remember:
There are good reasons for only having a small snack to break your fast before performing the evening prayer and then eating a bigger meal later. Muslim prayers involve a lot of movement — bending over, prostrating on the ground, standing up, etc. Doing all that physical activity on a full stomach after not having eaten for 15 hours is a recipe for disaster. Just trust me on this one.

Mosq (Musjid)

(Quran 5:3):
Today I have perfected your religion, and completed my favours for you and chosen Islam as a religion for you"

Mosq (Musjid)

(Quran 5:3):
Today I have perfected your religion, and completed my favours for you and chosen Islam as a religion for you"

Mosq (Musjid)

From the Prophet Farewell Sermon:
Fear Allah concerning women! Verily you have taken them on the security of Allah, and intercourse with them has been made lawful unto you by words of Allah.

Mosq (Musjid)

From the Prophet Farewell Sermon:
O people, listen to my words. I do not know whether I shall ever meet you again in this place after this year. O people, your blood and your property are sacrosanct until you meet your Lord, just as this day and this month of yours are sacred. Surely you will meet your Lord and He will question you about your deeds.

Mosq (Musjid)

From the Prophet Farewell Sermon:
Know for certain that every Muslim is a brother of another Muslim, and that all Muslims are brethren. It is not lawful for a person [to take] from his brother except that which he has given him willingly, so do not wrong yourselves. O God, have I not conveyed the message?" It was reported [to me] that the people said, "O God, yes," and the Messenger of God said, "O God, bear witness."

Mosq (Musjid)

From the Prophet Farewell Sermon:
O people, your Lord is One, and your father is one: all of you are from Adam, and Adam was from the ground. The noblest of you in Allah's sight is the most godfearing: Arab has no merit over non-Arab other than godfearingness. Have I given the message?—O Allah, be my witness. —At this, they said yes.

He said, Then let whomever is present tell whomever is absent.

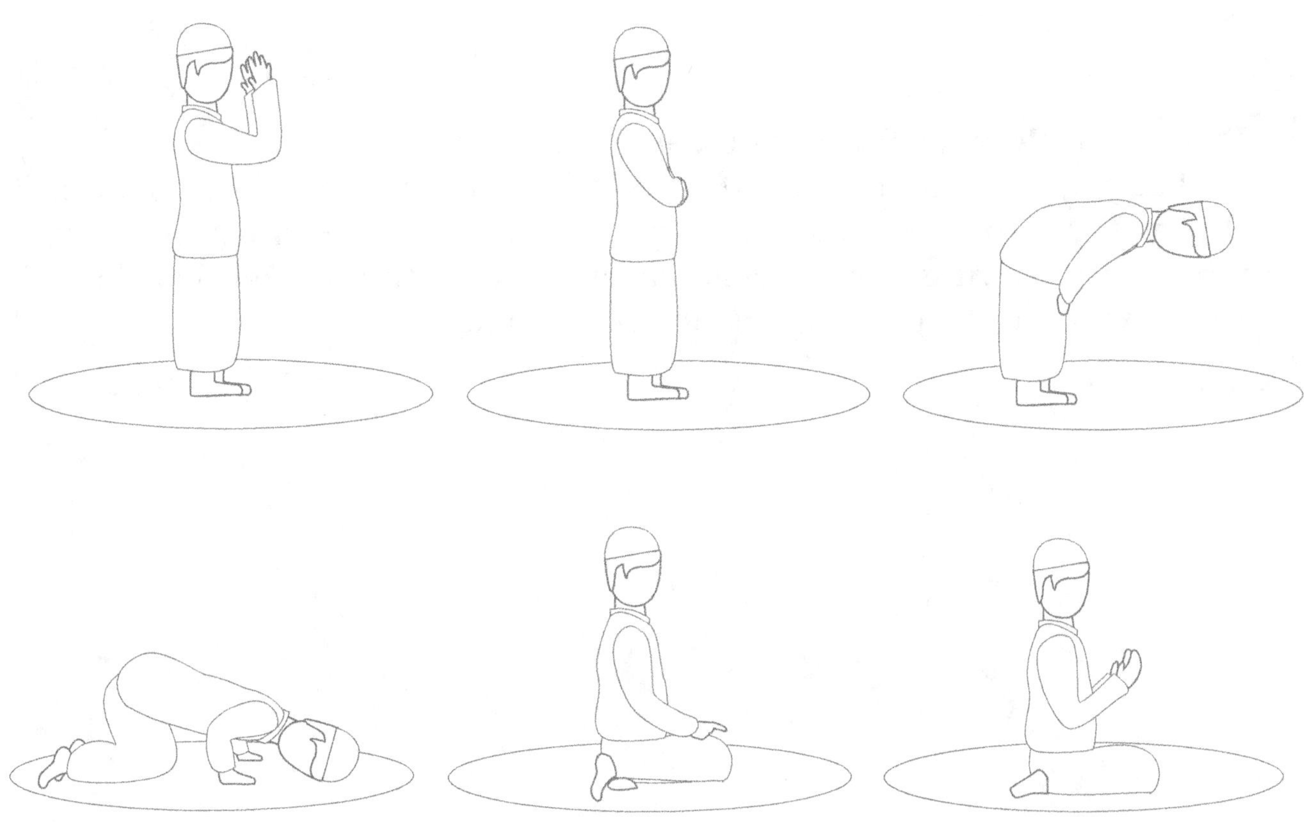

ALLAH
ALLAH
ALLAH
ALLAH
ALLAH

Islamic Mandala

From the Prophet Farewell Sermon:
All mankind is from Adam and Eve, an Arab has no superiority over a non-Arab nor a non-Arab has any superiority over an Arab; also a white has no superiority over black nor a black has any superiority over white except bypiety (taqwa) and good action. Learn that every Muslim is a brother to every Muslim and that the Muslims constitute one brotherhood. Nothing shall be legitimate to a Muslim which belongs to a fellow Muslim unless it was given freely and willingly. Do not, therefore, do injustice to yourselves.

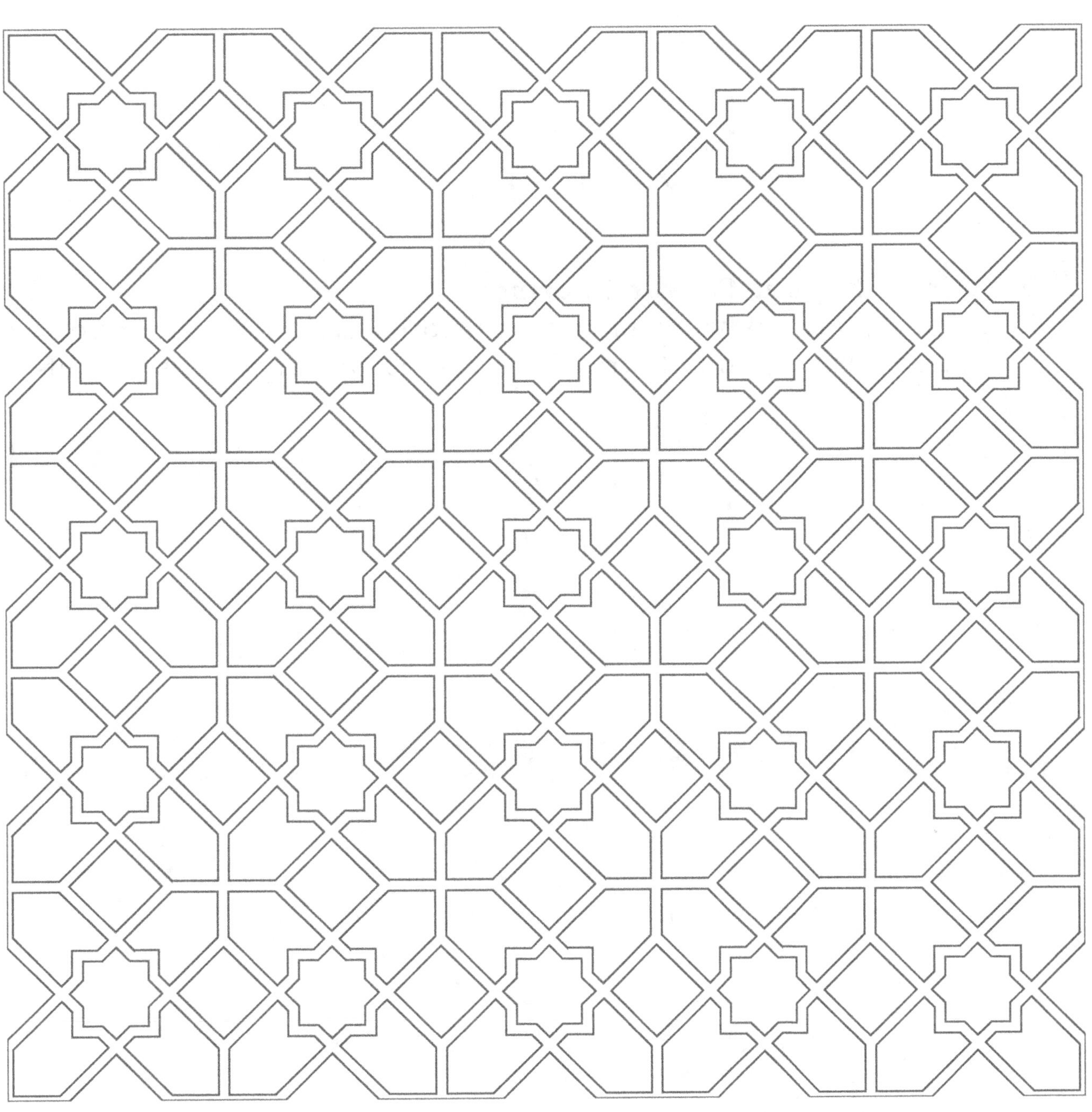

Islamic Mandala

Who is Muhammad (Peace Be Upon Him):
Born approximately 570 CE (Year of the Elephant) in the Arabian city of Mecca, Muhammad was orphaned at the age of six. He was raised under the care of his paternal grandfather Abd al-Muttalib, and upon his death, by his uncle Abu Talib. In later years, he would periodically seclude himself in a mountain cave named Hira for several nights of prayer. When he was 40, Muhammad reported being visited by Gabriel in the cave and receiving his first revelation from God.